Dedicated to my past self:

You didn't think I could do it.
How you feel now?
Don't you ever doubt me again

Dedicated to my father:

Everything I am, you were first.

I love you.

TABLE OF CONTENTS

PREYING MANTIS

I am 5 years old and obsessed with zoobooks
The stories of animals have always been more interesting than my
own

I am 2 years old and my mother is a praying mantis

I am 8 years old and my father is a headless rooster protecting his
nest
he may have lost his mind but his body still works hard, it's the
only thing he knows

I am 13 years old and my stepmother is a light at the end of the
tunnel
I am 15 years old and my stepmother has teeth
I am 17 years old, my stepmother is an angler fish
We so easily drawn to the light return to the darkness to escape
being devoured

I am 10 years old and my mother is an emperor penguin
during the worlds hardest winter
We huddle together to find warmth
While all of her visits begin and end with cold feet

I am 20 years old and I am a hermit crab learning to make a
temporary home in metaphors

I am 12 years old and all the women in my church
are hyenas laying their carcasses at our feet,
each one of them hungry for a chance to be the next queen
We run from their whimpers and laughter
Fully aware of their ability to chew through bone

I am 16 years old and I am a spider casting my web
so wide I can't tell when someone has actually caught on

I am 9 years old and my father is still a headless rooster trying to teach my
songbird sisters about the sky
though he knows he will never be able to fly

I am 28 years old and I still don't know any proper mating rituals Only to
hunt, to provide, to work

I am 28 years old and I'm still afraid of any woman
who takes control of my head too quickly

I am 28 years old and I am expected to treat my mother as a momma bear
like she didn't hibernate through all the winters,
most of the birthdays, the holidays,
both times I got my heart broken,
struggled with school, learned how to dress, drive, do laundry, iron

I am 28 years old and I love my mother
because I am not an animal

I am 28 years old and my mother is human
My stepmother is human
My father is human
My sisters are human

I am 28 years old
I am not an animal
But I am growing out of this shell
The process is exhausting
The most vulnerable i'll ever be
Breaking into the strongest me i've ever **seen**

Lion Cub

Do not worry about making friends
They will come and go like breathing
Your lungs will hold onto the best ones and call them oxygen

Do not worry about your arms
Or envy your fathers strength
They are your birthright
Study his heart
It will take more years to learn his love
And it is the one thing that will get you through the worst times

Do not worry about words
I know they are sharp
I know they slice thought self-esteem like a knife
Make a mockery of your might
But one day they will be your greatest weapon
Love them and they will grow alongside your mane,
proud, wild, powerful

Young Kito
Look at this world
Everything the light touches was made by God
There will come a day when he sends you to the darkest places
Make sure they know the warmth of the son
And your roar will stretch across the Savannah
You will run opposite the stampede and not be trampled

Do not worry about your vision
Your eyes will be scarred by screens
They will make sure you see the obscene
Your brothers roasting in desert heat
Buzzards boasting over their rotting meat
Don't be surprised if they offer you a piece

Young Kito
I know how badly you want to be king
But our culture is not cannibal

We don't need to tear down another's rock to show our pride
You don't need riches to be a king
You don't need to "get girls" to be a king
You don't need a degree to be a king

Your royalty was gifted
Infused in your genes
YOU are the proof and product of survivors
Your DNA came from those who refused to be extinct
When the droughts would never end
When the world was split in half
When our fathers were stripped from the pride

You are here
Do not worry of the doom that looms over tomorrow
We have survived so many yesterday's
Store them away
You will call them faith
You will call them fate

TIGER

Ain't you that black?
Ain't you that nicey black?
Ain't you that bring this one round your white friends black?
Ain't your smile disarming?
Ain't you unarmed?
Ain't your Bible your sword?

Ain't you that, turn the other cheek type of cat?
Well ain't you the tamed tiger of the circus?
Can't I push your buttons without shorting your circuits?
I bet you jump through rings of fire on command.
Look at you!

Ol shadow-of-your-former-self face ass
Your skin used to be camouflage
What you hunting now nigga?

You just blend in with the rest of the black
Ol fake t'challa lookin ass
Strip away your armor and you just another nigga!

Ol domesticated cat lookin ass
You only share your ancestors eyes
You don't share your ancestors drive
You didn't share their struggle,
So you don't share their strength
You mistake a ball of yarn for oppression
You mistake a cracked whip for brutality
You ain't in danger
'less you step out yo place
Just balance on your balls nigga
You got no reason to fall!!

8

What you gonna do?
You just gon walk away?

Fine with me nigga,
You can't escape
Can't escape
You can't..
You...
Nig-...
T.... ....
You.......
O-.........
OMG
You are SO talented!
Do another one of those BLACK poems!
You remind me of my friend roscoe!
Where can i find more of your work!?
Tell us your story!!..............nigga.

PANTHER

Sometimes I wish I was an animal,
Learning everything on instinct
Like no matter how much I fail I'll learn to fly

If I could
I'd ask the eagle if he ever doubted himself leaning over the edge of
the nest
the monkey if he ever thought he wouldn't be able to climb
After the first few failed attempts at a hunt,
Did the panther,
Another gazelle wrenching itself free from his grasp,
feel like quitting?

"If you ain't learned to hunt "
said the panther,
"you ain't been hungry enough"

The current is waiting to sweep them away
to her children knowinging
She gives her body
How can I
She cries and I don't blame her
She lashes out and I don't blame her
She mourns and I don't blame her
Or sink to the ocean floor
wash up on the beach
She cannot feast while the bones of her sisters
The current is quiet but she has no peace
she reaches the top of the river
She just swims and somehow
Wriggles from the waiting jaws of a bear
Narrowly escapes the clutches of an eagle
She leaps and is greeted by every manner of predator
The white water tells her stay down
The white water thrashes at her audacity
And the current becomes rapids
so she decides to swim
All are the wrong options
It says don't be lazy
The current says stay at home
But don't focus too much on your career
The current says do twice the work, get half as much
Her tailfin is an ungodly work ethic
Her Dorsal fin is a degree
Up the stream to work
So she decides to swim
All are wrong options
The current says cut it off or perm it, braid it or burn it
But the current says it's not enough for her to be beautiful
Her hair will listen to her today
Jump out of bed early in the morning
she doesn't know any other way to swim
She's been fighting the current so long
Her Magic Makes the waves seem irrelevant
Commander of ocean and river
How she transitions from salt to fresh water so seamlessly
I love her more than anything but i'll never understand her
The Salmon is my Sister

SALMON

CRAB

They say we be like crabs in a bucket
A brother said
"Why are the crabs in a bucket in the first place?"
The bucket is not his natural habitat
Some crabs like open ocean
Some hide under a rock if they choose, but they choose it
Crabs only fight when their resources are limited
Stuffed into a space too small to live in
Someone had to have taken the crab from its home
Put it in a bucket
Wrapped up its claws
Told it everything beautiful comes from outside the bucket
God forbid they learn to love it
Treat it like a fish tank, make it a home
They dump the crabs out and give it to creatures more worthy
God forbid they get out the bucket
Their reward is a bath of boiling water
A chorus of cackling cameras cheering on their descent
Soft Insides and hard shell
Just the way they like us
Easy to butter up
Easy to devour
They say we be like crabs in a bucket
That's funny
Cuz wouldn't that make them human

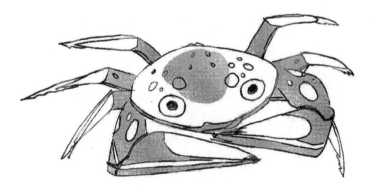

KOMODO DRAGON

The Komodo dragon wants so badly to breathe fire
He has none
This dragon wanted power
But he had none
It wasn't enough for him to be the biggest lizard
To be so engorged on all the food he would ever need
This dragon wanted to be mythical
He wanted to fly to terrorize anyone he thought peasant
To burn barren lands to the crisp
Pretend those lands weren't also his own
He wanted to burn a wall around the best spots to bask in the sun
He was cold-blooded
Yet could not measure the temperature of a room
If you ask him he would deny the heat of the sun
Blame the death of eggs on slimmer lizards
Ignore the cannibalism of other male dragons like him
But the dragon had no "real" power

The dragon told a tale of poison
He beat his chest and hissed at protest
Fake news oozed from the side of his mouth
His stubby claws trampled over truth
Ruthless
He made a name by maiming the toothless
Fed fear to the foolish
Other dragons followed hoping to steal a bite from his carcass
A chorus of comrades circled the sky
Knowing his prey was soon to die
He did not hide his scales
He did not cover his claws
He bared his teeth
We could see the meat lodged in his gums
The blood curdled in his saliva
We could smell the racism on his breath
And yet

13

We gave him wings
We gave him fire
We gave him a house
We let him believe his power was a real

Komodo dragons are not fast
Komodo dragons are not a stealth hunters
Komodo Dragons do not have the stamina for a long battle
As far as we know Komodo dragons do not have venom
But what they do have is just as dangerous
It is believed that the mouth of a
Komodo dragon is so vile
So filled with bacteria, pathogen and germs
That it can kill with a single untreated bite

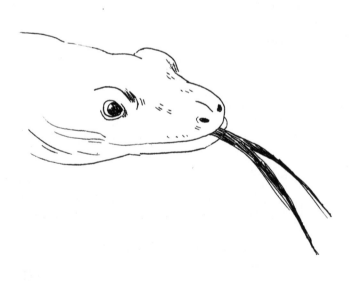

SERPENT

Most days I know the enemy by face
An unmistakable gait, his waltz like fire
Spelling destruction but so hard to look away

When you are a baby, the word "HOT" has no meaning to you
Temperature can only be measured but heat must be felt before you understand, understand
that I know the enemy by face and some days I let the devil win

I have walked bold face into the hurricane
hoping to find something in the eye
And return all sullen palm tree and broken damns

Is my city worth more to you now?
Will you gentrify rumors on my open ended sins?
Would you believe me?
If I told you I'm sober and still a virgin would you believe me?
Or are my white collar crimes less worthy of a burning?
Does it make a difference to dive into the pool without goggles or wings to keep me afloat?
Is a God a spiteful lifeguard?
On the days I let the devil win is my drowning a rejoice for the angels?

There are days when I choose the road most traveled because everyone else seems to return unscathed
My family told me it would be filled with monsters
With mistakes waiting to strip the flesh from my bones
But all I see are people with scars shaped different than mine
There are days when the right thing feels like
Einstein's definition of insanity
Doing the same thing over and over expecting something different
Days when I stand at the base of the mountain and scream hoping the avalanche will bury me alive or make me cold enough to survive

I've heard that in the time of ignorance God winks
but what if know better?

15

What if God sees me with eyes wide open?
Does that close the door for on my salvation?
Does that elevate me in the court of public opinion?

This Is not a call to glorify my wrongs
This is not an altar to sacrifice myself for the culture
This is my final stand against myself
To say there are days i let the devil win but this is not one of them

He is a cunning serpent
We are all in the tallgrass likely to be bitten
But never forget that the devil wins more often
when we pretend like he doesn't
Having poison filled bodies, acting like we're fine
Seeing poison filled bodies, ignoring the signs
Point our noses to the sky like a herd of self righteous unicorns
knowing damn well that pure unblemished creatures do not exist
on this earth

How many friends are we going to lose over mistakes?
Allies over arguments?
Leaders over unsuccessful relationships?
How many people will we let get bitten while we keep our pain to
ourselves?

I am a man with enough sins to be crucified 1000 times over
On my worst days I've had the kind of thoughts that would make a
demon blush and shudder in his boots
But all of my shortcomings become a hallelujah
All of my wrongs are a praise to god when I say
I will not let the devil win
Today

GIRAFFE

From up here we can see everything
Vertebrae a staircase to heaven
Our crown sits closer to God
We rubs shoulders on the weekends
If you ask nicely i'll put in good word for you

From up here
We can see everything
Not one sin gets past mine eye
Up here I can see your lies
Up here we have cut ties with the the common man
Up here we stand for something more

Every time I come down to earth there a rush of blood to my head
I have a 26 pound heart you know
It is filled to the brim with love
We are a peaceful people

O you mean these horns?
No need to worry
These are only for board meetings and crusades

Interesting

Normally we are so high up
No one seems to notice

G.O.A.T.

I wanted to be like Mike till I found out he owns prisons
I wanted a mamba mentality till
I realized sometimes quitting is the right thing
I wanted to be like Tiger till he refused to acknowledge his stripes
I wanted to dance like Michael till the lost boys told stories of Neverland

Lately I have trouble believing anyone can fly
All of the stars come crashing down to earth and i question
How God even gave them a chance to sparkle
I am but a newborn ball of light
What hope do i have if all of my role models could not escape
the black hole?
Will the next generation see all the bones in my wardrobe?
Turn it into coffin
Bury me with all those lessons we pretend we didn't learn from the cosby
show
The songs we pretend don't have our best memories attached to them

I have never seen a billy goat without a bit of grey in its beard
Been on this earth long enough to see that human perfection is both the
Lord's plan and the Devil's lie
I know that once a painter begins
Some mistakes can be covered by colors and others call for the canvas to
be thrown out

I don't know what kind of life I'm making here
but I am hoping not to be a complete waste of paper
I am pushing to make sure the next generation will not regret learning
from me
And somehow still embrace the irony of who inspired me to climb
mountains in the first place
Who taught me to taught me to put my head down and charge forward
fearless

Can I be the difference?
Can I be the one to pull some of that light out the black hole without being sucked in?
Can i flatten out a crumpled canvas to see if there is value in the color schemes?
I'm not a Kid anymore
I wear my sins on the crown of my head hardened from constant battles
I tell myself I want to be the Greatest of all time
But I sense I Will be slaughtered for showing my horns

HONEY BADGER

And I told her
You are the marrow in my bones, my most precious resource

I told her
You are the yoga instructor of my time, my muse
The molding of my metaphors

And I told her, tell me anything
That I would keep her secrets in the safest place
Her desires locked in my adamantium atrias
Her fears silenced in my vibranium ventricles
No one can reach them without the spilling of blood

I told her
I would never need a compass
That I could spot her smile from the outer edge of the Milky Way

And I told her
That I've never been in love, but
If it was only as good as her fingers in my afrol'd understand
God all the same

And I told her
That I'm not perfect
That I write things down because i'm terrible at thinking on my feet
That I got mommy issues
Like I still can't cut a block of cheese in a straight line

That according to everyone I'm supposed to finish last
Probably because my insecurities glued my starting blocks to the
bottom of my cleats
But I still keeping running, awkward and clunky
because she might be the first finish line I'd lose a thousand races for

And I told her
All I want is a chance to make these more than metaphors
All I can ask for is a chance to love you

……..but the honey badger didn't give a shit.

Parrot

Nobody:
Men in my family: Hey black child!
Me: Hey black child!
Men: Do you know who you are? Who you really are?
Me: Do you know who you are? Who you really are?
Men: You are strong!
Me: I am strong!
Men: You have the ability to do anything!
Me: I have the ability to do anything!
Men: Say no to drugs!
Me: Say no to drugs!
Men: He who finds a wife, finds a good thing!
Me: He who finds a wife, finds a good thing!
Men: Be careful, make sure she really loves you!
Me: Be careful, make sure she really loves you!
Men: God is good!
Me: God is good!
Men: all the time!!
Me: all the time!!
Nobody:
Men: FYAH BUN ANTI-MAN!!!

Me:
Men: These black Americans lazy inno!
Me:
Men: Dat poetry en makin money boy!
Me:
Men: How many girl you have by D house?
Me:
Men: When i was you age! I had tree children already!
Me:
Men: You know the problem with allyuh generation?
Me:
Men: Allyuh don listen!!
Me: We listen.

OWL

Everyone knows owls are nocturnal
Some say it's because God made them that way,
Others say they adapted to hunting at night to avoid larger
predators
I say it's a bit of both

All I know is
They're super dope

Did you know they have ridiculously sensitive hearing
and night vision?
Like James Bond?

Did you know they fly completely silent?
Like a gah damn ninja bird?

They don't have wet poop
They cough up furry pellets with the bones of their food inside
Like a present! Owls are Santa Claus!
Astronaut Santa claus!

Did you know they have one of the strongest grips in animal
kingdom?
450 lbs of force per square inch

I've always wanted to be awesome like
My favorite super-dope-james bond-astronaut-Santa Claus-
death grip-Ninja Bird!

Completely adapted to dominate the night like Batman

But I am an owl who's afraid of the dark

waking up in my father's shadow
Born for greatness but always
Fearing the very thing I was raised under

fighting my fiercest ally
too often fighting sleep when the rest of my kind are working
I am observing from the trees
I should be hunting

My family is full of folks with innocent faces
that cloak our destrutive potential
What good is inheriting my father's talons without his killer instinct?
What good is knowing the power that rests in my hands
without the desire to squeeze out that last inch of life?
What good Is having a vision
if I can't see the route to reach my goal?

These days, my flight feels more like a free fall,
wings folded at my sides
enjoying the rush of wind before the inevitable earth claims me

And I wonder
Am I just avoiding the larger predators
or did God make me this way
And if God made me this way,
would he let an owl starve while his eye is on the sparrow?

And I remember
that an owls' ears are so excellent
they can often hunt with hearing alone
never seeing the prey before it's already in their grasp

And I wonder if I close my eyes
let go of my foothold and listen
If my trust my master's engineering
I wonder what I could do with these hands?

ROTTWEILER

I am a Rottweiler with dreadlocks
I am jerk chicken and chicken and waffles
I'm a jerk and I know cuz bad man nah fake friend
I am salt on mangoes but never salty
I am jerk chicken and chicken and waffles
A bass speaker for a heart
I am salt on mangoes but never salty
A steel pan for a soul
A bass speaker for a heart
Everywhere is my home
A steel pan for a soul
I don't belong here
Everywhere is my home
My teeth cut cane better than my ancestors
I don't belong here
We are God's first flowers with no fear of the sun
My teeth cut less cane than my ancestors
I'm a jerk and I know cuz bad man nah fake friend
We are God's first flowers with no fear of the sun
I am a Rottweiler with dreadlocks

WOLF

Today I told my student I love him
He had no idea what to do with himself
He's been in camp for 9 months
Hasn't seen anything past these walls
His only glimpse once a week in my class when he gets to spit bars
From 8s to 16's each is a means to catch a gleam of the outside world
He sings hoping someone can hear the hollow in his howl

The forest calls him monster
Say he only hunt
Snow bunnies call him a dog
Say he only fuck
He too wild to have a home
I say he was never made to live in a cage
I say he only dangerous when he's cornered
I say they watch too much YouTube or Worldstar or Nat Geo
A young colored man goes to jail and all of a sudden
Everyone becomes David Attenborough
Try to narrate his life
Pretend to care
Pretend they been there
Like they know what its like to live in a wolfpack
where everyone who aint an alpha don't eat
So every chance he get he bares teeth
Every chance he get he bangs beats
The rhythm reminds him of a simpler time
A puppy who just opened his eyes
His only responsibility was to eat and play
Not worry where his food is coming from today

And he's still a puppy
Yet to find his voice
Asked to lead the hunt

So We rock like jay rock
Chill like meek mill
Spit like Kendrick and the kick drum numbs the pain
A few seconds of solace in a place where silence can send you insane
A few moment of music to mix up the mundane
A few bars to boast the brilliance he never knew he had in his brain

I bet you didn't know that wolf puppies are born deaf
I bet you didn't know that lone wolves howl longer and louder than one at home
I bet you didn't know that in a wolfpack the only thing that breaks the mourning of lost members is the arrival of new puppies

It seems to me the wolves had discovered something we haven't
That Maybe if we have taught him how to use his voice earlier he wouldn't have been lost in the first place
That even if he's lost he can still be beautiful
That when a member is lost we don't stop singing till we bring the next generation home

He was raised in a Wolfpack
Knows respect when he hears it
He smells fear
He just wants to know that someone will sit through the snarls
Listen to the growls
Hold a few painful bites
And not run away
I tell him "I love you man"
he says nothing
But shows me all of his teeth the only way he knows how

THE ZOO

Mateo is a capuchin who lives at the zoo where I work
Every time I pass by his cage he runs up, jumps on the fence,
presses his face to the links and screams
When I turn my head one way he turns his too
I walk one way, he follows
I think we're friends but I'm pretty sure if he ever got out he'd rip
my face off
The gibbons are my favorite
They wake up early in the morning swinging and singing to their
heart's content long before the guests ever get there
I'm always shocked at how such a beautiful harmony can come
from a monkey
The rough necked lemurs are quiet most of the time but at any
given moment they can go crazy and growl
it sounds like they are fighting but they rarely ever do
It just sounds like it
The spider monkeys pretend to be sweet but are actually quite
vicious
If you turn your back to them, they'll reach through the fence
and snatch you up

People come to the zoo to see things they've never seen before
To observe the amazing while being at a safe distance
They point and laugh and joke and smile
Great for the whole family

Most days I avoid the people like the plague
But Today I am working inside an exhibit
My brain does everything to keep a grip on reality
To be present
But I always know when the little white babies have never seen a
black man before
Their confusion, their astonishment, their admiration
How they have never seen gold in this hue
Never seen skin that reminds them of sun's power
Hair that raises praise to its creator

Today
I can't unsee it
100 years ago I could have been an attraction here

Today the children see a man in a cage
They point and laugh and joke and smile
The parents watch from a safe distance
They look at me the same way I look at Mateo

Like I would rip their faces off if I got the chance
Like I can snatch them up with my back turned
or with my hands up
or white knuckled on a steering wheel
No wonder they are so eager to keep us caged
They see us on tv only when we go crazy and growl
When it seems like we are fighting and we certainly do
But in the morning
We get up singing to our hearts content when no one else is around
Finding harmony in our God and with our people

I no longer work at the zoo
But I still feel caged in a grocery store
at Disneyland
on stage

And most days, like many zoo animals, I learn to love the attention
I pick my fro as far as it will reach
I laugh like the jokes are funny
I press my face to the cage and turn my head the way I want me to

And other days I am consumed with what is missing
I pace back and forth
Frantically, dangerously
An image of my homeland itching the under of my cranium
and I can't reach it, just thinking
I. don't. belong. here.

My brain does everything to keep a grip on reality
To be present
To say I will not be caged if I don't want to
I will not apologize for finding an escape here
And I will never stop demanding for a better home
Either in a scream, in a growl, or in a song

Thanks and Acknowledgements

Hannah Bosnian - Illustrator/Editorial Design
Kesha Lake
Shondelle & Joseph Fortune
Robert "Bird" Lopez
Daniel Holder
Alyesha Wise & Mathew "Cuban" Hernandez
Da Poetry Lounge Family
Daniel Lisi
Garrick Bernard
Dave Richardson
Lance Hundley
Travis Basabas
New Earth Organization
Mt. Rubidoux SDA Church Family
Anthony Depree

I love you all, and I am SO grateful!

All praise be the All Mighty God, my big homie and ghost-writer

Made in the USA
Middletown, DE
16 May 2020